Splashdown

Story by Mike Lefroy

Illustrations by Liz Alger

For Bill Bell, whose adventures
inspired this story.

Rigby PM Plus Chapter Books
part of the Rigby PM Program
Ruby Level

U.S. edition © 2003 Rigby Education
A division of Reed Elsevier Inc.
1000 Hart Road
Barrington, IL 60010 - 2627
www.rigby.com

Text © 2003 Thomson Learning Australia
Illustrations © 2003 Thomson Learning Australia
Originally published in Australia by Thomson Learning Australia

10 9 8 7 6 5 4 3 2
07 06 05 04

Splashdown
    ISBN 0 75786 894 0

Printed in China by Midas Printing (Asia) Ltd

Contents

Chapter 1   Night Take-off   4

Chapter 2   Pacific Dawn   8

Chapter 3   Emergency   11

Chapter 4   Splashdown   15

Chapter 5   Drifting   20

Chapter 6   Signs of Life   23

Chapter 7   The Silver Lining   27

Chapter 8   Liftoff   31

Chapter 1
Night Take-off

"Ready?" Uncle Bill asked.

"Ready!" replied Cassie, sucking in her breath and bracing herself against the seat.

Uncle Bill turned the key. The engines started with a cough and the small cabin shook like a wet dog. Cassie watched her uncle's face glowing in the dim light. His hands danced over the instrument panel. The speed and certainty of his actions gave her a feeling of comfort and safety.

Uncle Bill released the brake and the plane slowly began rolling down to the runway.

Finally they turned and stopped. Cassie could see a long corridor of lights stretching into the blackness.

It was the night before her twelfth birthday and this was Cassie's special treat. She had been pestering her mother for some time to be allowed to fly to the island with Uncle Bill.

"You go, why can't I?" she had said.

"When you're twelve," was her mother's reluctant promise at her last birthday.

Just last week Uncle Bill called to say he had a plane to deliver to a new owner on the island, and asked if anyone would like to come along for the ride. Cassie worked on her mother for three days until she finally agreed to letting her go.

At last a voice crackled in the cockpit. It was the OK from the control tower.

They were on their way.

Uncle Bill looked across at his young co-pilot and gave a quick thumbs up.

His hand went to the throttles, and he steadily moved them upward. The engines roared, the plane surged forward, and Cassie felt herself sinking back into her seat. Outside, the lights flashed past, and then suddenly they were airborne.

The plane climbed steeply then banked slowly to the left. Below, Cassie could see the lights of the city shaping roads and houses.

Ahead of them there was nothing.

"The sea!"

The noise was overwhelming but Cassie could lip-read Uncle Bill's words as he pointed through the windshield.

She remembered their conversation as they were walking to the plane. Cassie had flown with Uncle Bill many times before, but this was her first night flight. He had explained that the late take-off meant they could fly all night and land in daylight.

"The first part will be dark and noisy. Try to sleep and save yourself for the dawn. It really is beautiful over the water."

She put on her headphones, slipped a CD into her player, and settled back into her seat.

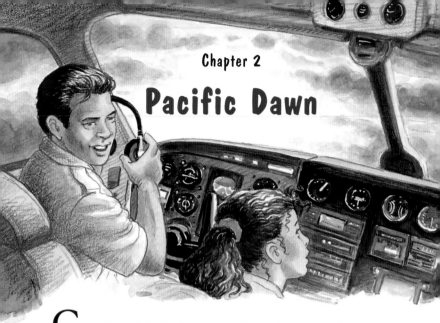

Chapter 2
Pacific Dawn

Cassie didn't know what it was that woke her. Perhaps it was the first streaks of light or maybe it was a slight change in engine noise. Whatever it was, she was suddenly wide awake.

"Hi, sleepy head. Happy birthday!" said Uncle Bill, removing his headset.

"Where are we?" she asked.

Uncle Bill picked up a clipboard from beside the seat and pointed to the map.

"Here. About half way. Sleep well?"

"Yes, fine," yawned Cassie.

"Just going to switch fuel tanks, and then we can have something to eat," said Uncle Bill.

There was a stutter from an engine and Uncle Bill's hand flashed back to the instrument panel. He tapped a gauge and flicked the fuel tank switches. Cassie sensed something wasn't quite right. Suddenly there was a second stutter and a choking sound. Cassie saw the propeller on her side changing from a blur to a slowly twirling blade. She looked across at Uncle Bill. He smiled at her, but only with his mouth. She could tell by his eyes that there was something wrong. When the other engine sputtered and slowed, she knew for sure.

It was suddenly very quiet. The horizon climbed upward through the windshield as the nose of the plane tilted down.

"We're going into a short dive," said Uncle Bill. "Hang on... shouldn't be long... just going to re-start these engines."

"Why have you stopped them?" asked Cassie, gripping her seat.

Uncle Bill didn't answer. He had done this trip many times, mostly by himself.

Never had any trouble before — why this time?

Just then the engines coughed and sputtered. The propellers blurred once more, and the plane leveled out.

Uncle Bill's shoulders relaxed as he let out a huge sigh.

"Better start climbing again," he said. He was really smiling now.

Chapter 3

Emergency

Cassie laid out the food on a tray between them. She handed Uncle Bill a sandwich.

"Everything should be fine now," he said, taking his hands off the controls. "We'll let the autopilot take us through breakfast."

Cassie carefully poured the last of the coffee into Uncle Bill's cup.

"Just put the thermos back in the cooler. We won't be needing that again this trip," said Uncle Bill. "Careful, it's made of glass," he said as he watched her screw the top back on it.

Cassie slipped a new CD into her player. She peeled herself a banana and was just settling back in her seat when it happened again. A stutter, a bang, and a sigh and the propellers suddenly appeared.

Uncle Bill grabbed the controls as the nose of the plane dipped. His half-eaten sandwich dropped onto the cockpit floor, spilling onto his shoes.

Cassie sensed this time it was really serious. She slipped off her headphones and watched as Uncle Bill's fingers darted across the panel in front of him with a frightening urgency. He spoke into his headset between nervous twists of the radio control button.

Cassie watched him for some sign of reassurance. But this time he didn't look across at her.

The noise from the engines had disappeared completely. It felt like they were floating. Cassie looked down at the sea below.

Uncle Bill took off his headset as the plane continued to glide down.

"We're going to have to land on the water," he said grimly.

"Won't we sink?" asked Cassie.

"No, it's like a boat. It will just ride on top. But we'll put on life jackets just in case."

Uncle Bill pulled out two packages from under the seats. He put his life jacket on, encouraging Cassie to copy him. She gulped down her banana and slipped into her jacket.

Uncle Bill glanced across and tried a reassuring smile, but Cassie was just looking straight ahead, willing the plane to stay up.

"Any second now I'm going to stick the nose right up in the air. It'll slow us down just before we land."

Cassie hugged her jacket and nodded.

"As the nose goes up, the tail will catch the water and we'll just bellyflop down," continued Uncle Bill. "Then we'll step onto the wing. I'll launch the life raft…"

"But I want to stay in the plane," said Cassie. "I don't want to get into a raft." She was beginning to panic.

Chapter 4

Splashdown

"Hang on!" Uncle Bill shouted.

Just before she closed her eyes, Cassie glanced to her right. The water was coming toward them much too fast.

Uncle Bill wrenched the controls back. The windshield was suddenly full of sky, and Cassie felt her whole body trying to go backward through the seat. Then, just as quickly, she was jerked forward and felt her seat belt burning across her hips.

Then there was nothing.

"OK?" asked Uncle Bill, grabbing Cassie's arm.

"I... I think so..." Cassie looked up to see water running down the windshield.

Uncle Bill had his seat belt off quickly and was opening the door. He dragged a large white container out from the back of the plane and tied it to his seat before shuffling it onto the wing. He slid it into the water and to Cassie's amazement it broke open to reveal an orange rubber life raft.

"Right, let's get the rest of breakfast," said Uncle Bill.

While he perched on the wing, Cassie passed the cooler out to him. Uncle Bill held the floating raft beside the plane with his foot and then carefully lowered the cooler inside.

"Now, time to hop in." Uncle Bill stood up on the wing, feet spread apart to balance, and reached his hand into the plane.

Cassie shrank back into her seat. She didn't want to leave. Uncle Bill realized it was not going to be easy. He stood up and looked around to gather his thoughts. Just out to the north he noticed a build-up of clouds.

That's a bit of weather heading our way, he thought grimly to himself. They had to get into the life raft before it hit them.

"You'll need your CD player and your jacket," he said as calmly as he could. Cassie still didn't move. She sat hugging herself tightly, staring out the windshield.

"CASSIE! NOW!"

The spell was broken. She swung around quickly and looked at her uncle.

"Your hand," he said, giving her no choice. He guided her onto the wing and then bent down to retrieve the rope of the life raft. Cassie clung tightly. She felt the first gust of wind on her face.

"My CD player!" she said, and suddenly let go of Uncle Bill's hand. He stumbled forward and fell head first onto the edge of the raft. Cassie watched in horror as the raft flipped high into the air and flopped down in the water beside her uncle. The capsized raft swung sideways and the rope, still attached to the plane, sliced across her legs and knocked her into the water.

Chapter 5

Drifting

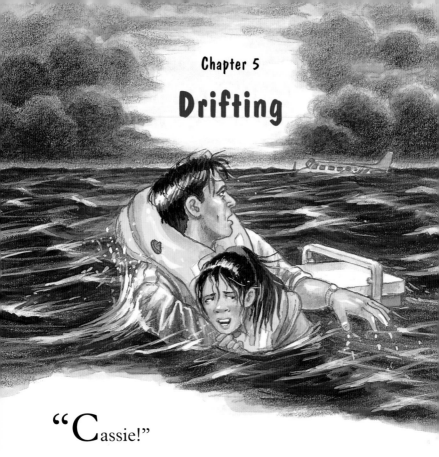

"Cassie!"

She heard the cry as she broke the surface.

"Pull the cord on the front!"

She tugged the string on the front of her life jacket and felt herself pop up in the water as the jacket inflated itself. Uncle Bill, floating beside her, attached himself to her with a rope.

Cassie tried to brush the hair out of her face but the wind was too strong. Her eyes were stinging from the salt water.

She looked around for the life raft, but it was drifting away, still attached to the plane.

"Don't worry, this won't last long," shouted Uncle Bill over the sound of the wind.

"Turn your back to the waves," he said, putting his arm around her shoulder.

Cassie suddenly felt very small and very alone. She buried herself into Uncle Bill's arm and burst into tears.

★ ★ ★

The squall was quickly over and the peaceful morning returned.

"Let's have some food while we're waiting for a lift home," said Uncle Bill. "I've saved a few things," he said, clutching the cooler which was floating beside them.

"Does anyone know we're here?" Cassie asked.

"I've set off two emergency beacons," said Uncle Bill. "Someone will have picked up our message and will be on their way right now."

"Are you sure?" she asked.

"Yes, I'm sure," he replied.

What he didn't say was that both the beacons were floating away from them. One was in the plane and the other firmly attached to the life raft. The squall had driven the plane, with the life raft in tow, well away from them. Uncle Bill looked over Cassie's head at a smudge of white and orange in the distance. The plane and the life raft were still afloat and drifting. They would never be able to reach them now.

He realized that staying calm was their only hope.

Chapter 6
Signs of Life

They had eaten some of the oranges, and the sun was warming them up. Uncle Bill was fast running out of ideas. They'd sung all the songs they knew, played *Who Am I?* and even planned Cassie's twelfth birthday party.

"As soon as we get picked up, I'll radio ahead for a birthday cake. What kind would you like?" asked Uncle Bill.

But Cassie didn't answer.

"I spy…" Uncle Bill suddenly began. He had spotted a black shape just above the horizon. "With my little eye… something…"

"Plane!" shouted Cassie. She had heard the noise and swung her head around.

They both watched in silence as the dark shape transformed to a glowing silver plane. Then as it approached them, it banked to the south.

"They're heading for our plane," said Uncle Bill under his breath.

"They didn't see us!" cried Cassie.

"HELP!" she shouted desperately.

Silently he cursed himself for not tying one of the rescue beacons onto his life jacket.

      ★   ★   ★

Cassie was eating an orange. She was very quiet.

Uncle Bill continued to scan the sky to the west, the direction of the island, willing another spot to appear on the horizon. His head was aching from the sun, and his eyes were stinging from the salt water.

He looked at his watch. It was now nearly nine hours since they had splashed down. Suddenly he felt Cassie's hand raking his cheek.

"W... What's that?"

Uncle Bill swung around to see a huge tail lazily flicking out of the water nearby.

Neither of them spoke as an immense barnacled head slowly rose above the surface beside them. A rush of air and a spout of water broke the silence. The smell was overwhelming.

Uncle Bill realized he was nearly strangling Cassie as he clutched her to his side.

He looked across at her. Her face was frozen in a silent scream. A large eye broke the surface in front of them and held their gaze. Cassie could see the yellow of their life jackets reflected in it. Then the whale slowly sank out of sight, and they felt a surge of water as the huge mammal slid beneath them.

Cassie and Uncle Bill watched as the ripples slowly disappeared.

Neither of them spoke for a long time.

"We should have jumped on for a ride home," said Uncle Bill. He felt he had to say something, but immediately regretted it when he saw the tears.

"I just want to go home," Cassie sobbed.

Chapter 7

The Silver Lining

The sun was now low in the sky. The clouds to the west were long streaks of gray and pink smeared across the horizon. Uncle Bill knew it was a critical time. The chances of them lasting the night were very slim. Instinctively he pulled his knees up to his chest. Cassie was slowly eating the last orange. Now the only things left in the cooler were a couple of soaked granola bars and the empty thermos.

Cassie heard it first.

"Over there! Over there!" her voice exploded in his ear.

Uncle Bill swung around and saw the helicopter above the western horizon.

"The plane! They're heading for our plane again!" Uncle Bill was desperate now and he didn't try to hide it. He knew it was their last chance.

"We're here!" Cassie was losing her voice.

"Here!" Uncle Bill waved his arms and kicked his legs vigorously, trying to get higher out of the water.

Cassie slapped the water in despair as the helicopter continued to bank slowly to the south in search of their plane. Her arm smashed into the side of the cooler, spilling its contents into the water. The empty thermos tumbled out and thumped Uncle Bill in the face. He grabbed it angrily and shouted at Cassie. He was really losing it now. They both were.

Suddenly Uncle Bill stopped and began to try and unscrew the bottom of the thermos. He mumbled to himself as he fought to remove the cover.

"A reflector... we need a reflector... we need to signal them."

Finally the cover loosened and he quickly removed it. He threw the plastic cover away and held up the shiny glass inner tube high above his head. The evening sun sparkled from the mirrored surface.

"What are you doing now?" Cassie sobbed.

Uncle Bill didn't answer. He just kept shouting as loud as he could and thrusting the flask high above his head.

"Look here! Over here!"

Just as they thought it was gone, the black shape wheeled slowly toward them.

"They've seen us!" cried Cassie.

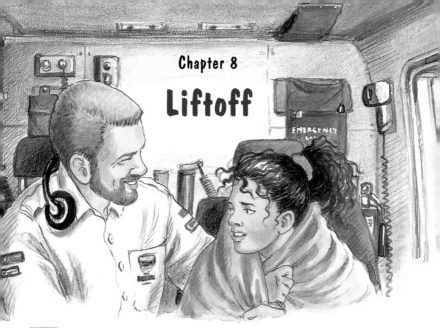

Liftoff

EMERGENCY

The noise inside the helicopter was deafening.

"How does that feel now?" shouted the man with a kind, bearded face into Cassie's ear as he wrapped another blanket tightly around her.

"You can thank old eagle-eyes Joe over there," he said, pointing to the figure beside the pilot. "He saw the flash of light as we were heading away from you."

Uncle Bill just nodded. He was still clutching the glass tube tightly in his hands.

"Is this your first ride in a helicopter?" asked the bearded man.

Cassie shivered, nodded, and smiled all at the same time as the helicopter leveled out and headed for the island.

Uncle Bill leaned over to his smiling niece.

"Now, about that birthday cake... what kind would you like?"